SRA Specific Skill Series
for Language Arts

Sentences

Leveled Books
in Nine Key
Language Arts Skill Areas

SRA

Columbus, OH

The McGraw-Hill Companies

Cover: ©Tim Flach/Getty Images, Inc.

SRAonline.com

SRA

Copyright © 2005 by SRA/McGraw-Hill.

All rights reserved. Except as permitted under the United States Copyright Act, no part of this publication may be reproduced or distributed in any form or by any means, or stored in a database or retrieval system, without the prior written permission of the publisher, unless otherwise indicated.

Send all inquiries to:
SRA/McGraw-Hill
8787 Orion Place
Columbus, OH 43240-4027

Printed in the United States of America.

ISBN 0-07-601715-X

2 3 4 5 6 7 8 9 MAZ 08 07 06 05

TO THE TEACHER

GENERAL INFORMATION ON SENTENCES

Writing complete, effective sentences requires an understanding of grammar, word meaning, and the conventions of punctuation. Native speakers of English use correct sentences in speech from an early age, showing that they grasp the concept of a sentence, even if they have not yet learned to transform their speech into written sentences and to correctly mark sentence boundaries. Nonnative speakers, however, often lack a sense of the sound and structure of a sentence in English; they may require a greater amount of exposure, both audible and visual, before they can begin to write correct, complete sentences consistently.

Common errors in student writing, such as run-ons, fragments, and comma splices, often occur as young writers experiment with new structures that will allow them to express more complex ideas. Instruction in sentence combining helps developing writers use more complex sentence structures.

ABOUT *SPECIFIC SKILL SERIES FOR LANGUAGE ARTS*

Specific Skill Series for Language Arts is a companion to ***Specific Skill Series,*** a supplemental reading program that has been widely recognized for its effectiveness for over thirty years. The two series are designed and organized the same. ***Specific Skill Series for Language Arts*** consists of discrete units of practice exercises that target and reinforce fundamental language-arts skills. Units in both series are presented in multiple-choice format for standardized test practice.

ABOUT *SENTENCES*

The scope and sequence for Books A through H of *Sentences* focuses on the grammatical elements of a sentence, sentence combining, and common sentence problems. The scope and sequence for each book is located on the last page of the book. Each unit includes

- **rule boxes** that explain concepts and rules related to sentence writing.
- **models** in each rule box to illustrate the concepts and rules.
- **multiple-choice exercises** for skills practice and reinforcement.

Four **Language Activity Pages** (LAPs) appear in each book. Each LAP is divided into the following four sections and reviews the skills practiced in the preceding units:

Exercising Your Skill reviews key terms and concepts.

Expanding Your Skill provides mixed practice.

Exploring Language shows how the skills apply to real-world contexts by featuring one of six forms of writing: descriptive, narrative, personal, persuasive, expository, and poetry.

Expressing Yourself includes two creative activities related to the skills. One activity is always a Work-with-a-Partner activity to encourage collaborative learning.

TO THE TEACHER

SERIES COMPONENTS

- **Student Editions:** Nine books in each level (A–H) focus on nine skill areas: *Grammar, Usage, Mechanics, Spelling, Vocabulary, Sentences, Paragraphs, Writing Process,* and *Research.*
- **Placement Test Books:** One book for each skill area includes diagnostic tests to place students in the correct level.
- **Teacher's Manual:** Primarily an answer key, the *Teacher's Manual* also includes reproducible student worksheets and further information on how to use the program, including classroom management tips.

HOW TO USE *SPECIFIC SKILL SERIES FOR LANGUAGE ARTS*

Placing Students in Levels: The scope and sequence, complexity of skills, and readability in Levels A through H correspond to Grades 1 through 8. Students may, however, be placed in any level. For example, in the second grade, a student who needs remedial work in a specific skill may be placed in Book A, an on-level student who would benefit from skills reinforcement may be placed in Book B, and an advanced student who is ready for enrichment may be placed in Book C or higher. *Placement Tests* help place students in the correct level.

Setting: This series can be used for independent study and one-on-one practice sessions, as well as in small-group and whole-class settings. It is also effective in after-school and summer-school programs.

Getting Started: Students must have notebook paper or copies of reproducible student worksheets (located in the *Teacher's Manual*) before they begin working. Remind students not to write in the books. Students may begin in any unit of any book, depending on the skill practice they need, although it is recommended that they begin with Unit 1. As they work through the units, students should record their answers on notebook paper or on the student worksheets.

Pacing: Students should be encouraged to work at their own pace, completing a few units every day or every other day.

Scoring: Teachers should score units as soon as they have been completed. Then a discussion can be held in which students justify their answer choices.

Internet Use: Some activities, especially those in *Research,* require students to use the Internet. Students' use of the Internet should be monitored closely for content appropriateness and safety.

TO THE STUDENT

Although you use sentences constantly when you speak and write, it is easy to make mistakes because there are so many rules for writing correct, complete sentences. This book will help you make fewer mistakes in your speech and written work.

In Book F *Sentences,* you will learn about

- Building Sentences
- Combining Sentences
- The Sound of Language
- Sentence Fluency
- Parallelism
- Sentence Problems
- Expanding Sentences

After you complete this book, you will be able to combine several sentences into one sentence that keeps the original meaning and is more fluent and interesting. One way to combine sentences is to use an appositive phrase.

Althea Gibson was a famous tennis player. She was the first African American to participate in the tournament at Wimbledon.

↓

Althea Gibson, a famous tennis player, was the first African American to participate in the tournament at Wimbledon.

Another way to combine sentences is to use a participial phrase.

Althea Gibson broke the color barrier in professional tennis. She paved the way for other African American tennis players.

↓

Breaking the color barrier in professional tennis, Althea Gibson paved the way for other African American tennis players.

You will also learn how to tell whether or not the parts of a sentence are parallel.

Not Parallel: Althea Gibson's goals were to beat the odds and winning tennis tournaments around the world.

Parallel: Althea Gibson's goals were **to beat** the odds and **to win** tennis tournaments around the world.

By mastering the skills in this book, you will know whether or not a sentence is complete and correctly punctuated. You will also know how to improve your sentences, which will improve your writing.

Unit 1
Building Sentences

Simple Subjects and Predicates

To build a complete sentence, you must have two main parts: a subject and a predicate. The subject tells *what* or *whom* the sentence is about. The predicate tells what the subject *does, is,* or *has*.

- A **simple subject** is the noun or pronoun that tells what the sentence is about. The **simple predicate** is the verb or verb phrase that expresses an action or a state of being about the subject of the sentence. A **verb phrase** consists of a main verb and all its helping verbs.

The **airplane is leaving** in twenty minutes.
(airplane = SIMPLE SUBJECT; is leaving = SIMPLE PREDICATE)

Furry and Fierce

Choose the simple subject or simple predicate that best completes each sentence.

1. The ______ (SUBJECT) attacks with its poisonous fangs.
   (A) quickly **(B)** tarantula **(C)** small

2. A tarantula can ______ (PREDICATE) prey with its powerful jaws.
   (A) unsuspecting **(B)** eyes **(C)** crush

3. ______ (SUBJECT) eat insects and frogs, and sometimes they even eat small birds.
   (A) They **(B)** Usually **(C)** Hide

4. Tarantulas in the wild often ______ (PREDICATE) in underground burrows.
   (A) very **(B)** hide **(C)** actually

5. The ______ (SUBJECT) wraps her fertilized eggs in a cocoon to protect them.
   (A) female **(B)** safely **(C)** later

6. Within two weeks of hatching, the young ______ (SUBJECT) leave the nest.
   (A) quickly **(B)** hungry **(C)** spiders

7. Young tarantulas ______ their skin about once a year until adulthood.
PREDICATE
(A) usually (B) shed (C) long

8. This ______ is called *molting*, and it also involves the regeneration, or renewal,
SUBJECT
of missing legs.
(A) process (B) sometimes (C) always

9. Thin strands of silk ______ like trip wires to let the tarantula know when
PREDICATE
prey is near.
(A) hidden (B) thin (C) work

10. Unlike most other spiders, ______ does not spin a web.
SUBJECT
(A) crawl (B) surprisingly (C) it

11. A cricket ______ a typical meal for a tarantula, even though it is capable of
PREDICATE
catching larger prey.
(A) they (B) is (C) and

12. ______ cannot be eaten whole, so the tarantula uses a substance it
SUBJECT
makes naturally to turn the insides of its prey into liquid.
(A) Food (B) Paralyze (C) Searching

13. Tarantulas ______ few natural enemies.
PREDICATE
(A) stomach (B) have (C) actually

14. ______ are known to prey on young tarantulas.
SUBJECT
(A) Scorpions (B) Venomous (C) Strike

Unit 2

Building Sentences

Complete Subjects and Predicates

When building sentences, you can also think in terms of complete subjects and predicates. The **complete subject** of a sentence includes the simple subject and any words that describe it. The **complete predicate** of a sentence includes the simple predicate and all the words that complete its meaning.

COMPLETE SUBJECT	COMPLETE PREDICATE
A cat's pupils	grow much larger in the dark.

- Don't mistake a subordinate clause as a complete subject or predicate even though it contains its own subject and predicate. A subordinate clause can be part of a complete subject or predicate, but it cannot exist in a sentence without being part of a subject or a predicate.

  Your cat cannot sit on the couch **until you brush her**.

- Also, don't be fooled by a participial phrase because it can neither be a complete subject nor a predicate. Even though it begins with a verb form, this kind of phrase usually describes something in the sentence and cannot stand alone.

  Sitting by the window, she looks so calm.

Famous Faces and Fictional Places

Choose the complete subject or complete predicate that best completes each sentence.

1. _____ followed the yellow-brick road in the Land of Oz to find the wizard.
   (A) Met the munchkins
   (B) To the Emerald City
   (C) With the help of her friends, Dorothy

2. The Wicked Witch of the West _____
   (A) melted when water was thrown on her.
   (B) and carrying her broomstick.
   (C) when Dorothy's house landed on her.

3. The legendary King Arthur's kingdom _____
   (A) a noble knight named Lancelot.
   (B) was called Camelot.
   (C) and the Knights of the Round Table.

4. _____ pulled the magic sword Excalibur from the stone.
   (A) In his youth
   (B) Guided by Merlin
   (C) Before he became king, a young Arthur

Unit 2
Building Sentences

5. ______ begin when she follows the white rabbit down a hole.
(A) At a tea party
(B) Alice's adventures in Wonderland
(C) Peering into the looking glass

---

6. The Cheshire Cat's grin ______
(A) remained after the rest of the cat had disappeared.
(B) on a tree limb.
(C) Alice was surprised.

---

7. *The Lord of the Rings* trilogy ______
(A) takes place in Middle Earth.
(B) in the peaceful Shire.
(C) from the wizard Gandalf.

---

8. ______ embark on a long journey to Mordor.
(A) With the help of the others
(B) Followed by Gollum
(C) The brave friends

---

9. In C. S. Lewis's famous stories, four kids from London ______
(A) the professor's old house.
(B) visit a place called Narnia.
(C) a lamppost in the woods.

---

10. ______ is the guardian of the children and the land of Narnia.
(A) Two-and-a-half thousand years later
(B) Created by Aslan
(C) The great lion

---

11. ______ live in a place called the Hundred-Acre Wood.
(A) The characters in Winnie-the-Pooh
(B) Visiting his friend Piglet
(C) A house for gloomy Eeyore

---

12. Winnie-the-Pooh author A. A. Milne ______
(A) of many different characters.
(B) named the character Christopher Robin after his own son.
(C) a collection of stories.

Unit 3
Building Sentences

Compound Subjects and Predicates

Sometimes you might have to use more than one subject or predicate when building a sentence because either two or more subjects do something or the subject does two or more actions.

- A **compound subject** is two or more simple subjects that have the same verb. Join the two related subjects with a conjunction, such as *and, or, neither/nor,* or *either/or*.

  Paige or **Letitia** will pick up the concert tickets.

- A **compound predicate** is two or more simple predicates that have the same subject. Connect the two related predicates with a conjunction, such as *and, but,* or *or*.

  Camilla **washed** and **peeled** vegetables for the stew.

- When choosing which conjunctions to use, remember that *and* means "added to" or "plus," *or/nor* means there is a choice of two or more, and *but* means "on the other hand," "in contrast," or "except."

Choose the best group of words to complete each sentence by forming a compound subject or a compound predicate.

1. Asia ______ are two of the world's seven continents.
   (A) and Africa
   (B) but Africa
   (C) or Africa

2. A computer either stores ______ information saved on its hard drive.
   (A) but retrieves
   (B) and retrieves
   (C) or retrieves

3. Cory remembered the flowers ______ the card.
   (A) or forgot
   (B) but forgot
   (C) nor forgot

4. Neither he ______ has ever heard of the book you are looking for.
   (A) nor she
   (B) but she
   (C) and she

5. Children's Day in Japan ______ are both celebrated on May fifth.
   (A) or Cinco de Mayo in Mexico
   (B) but Cinco de Mayo in Mexico
   (C) and Cinco de Mayo in Mexico

6. Greg either washes _____ the dishes after dinner.
   (A) and dries
   (B) but dries
   (C) or dries

7. The World Series _____ are two widely watched sporting events.
   (A) but the Super Bowl
   (B) and the Super Bowl
   (C) or the Super Bowl

8. Shawnna either rides her bike _____ to the park Saturday afternoon.
   (A) or walks
   (B) and walks
   (C) but walks

9. Kyoko was excited _____ when it was her turn to give her part of the presentation.
   (A) nor nervous
   (B) or nervous
   (C) but nervous

10. Georgio neither heard _____ anything out of the ordinary last night.
    (A) nor saw
    (B) and saw
    (C) but saw

11. Billy can sing _____ the guitar better than most people I know.
    (A) but play
    (B) and play
    (C) or play

12. The library _____ are both located on the same street downtown.
    (A) but the bank
    (B) nor the bank
    (C) and the bank

13. People remember _____ to a great leader of the civil rights movement on Martin Luther King Day.
    (A) and pay tribute
    (B) but pay tribute
    (C) nor pay tribute

Unit 3
Building Sentences

When building sentences with compound subjects and predicates, it is important to know when and where to use commas to separate the subjects or predicates.

- Do *not* use a comma in a compound subject made of only two subjects or a compound predicate made of only two predicates.

  Incorrect: Neither Mike, nor Elijah, wanted, or offered to help.

  Correct: Neither Mike nor Elijah wanted or offered to help.

- When a compound subject has more than two simple subjects, use a comma after each subject except for the last one.

  Gina**,** Alphonso**,** and I have to work on our report.

- When a compound predicate has more than two simple predicates, use a comma after each predicate except for the last one.

  We read**,** researched**,** and cited every bit of information.

Which is the correct way to form a compound subject or a compound predicate in each sentence below?

14. **(A)** A dress or a suit is often appropriate attire for some jobs.
    (B) A dress, or a suit, is often appropriate attire for some jobs.
    (C) A dress is often appropriate attire for some jobs or a suit.

15. **(A)** The outfielder bobbled, caught dropped the baseball in the final inning.
    (B) The outfielder bobbled caught, but then dropped, the baseball in the final inning.
    (C) The outfielder bobbled, caught, but then dropped the baseball in the final inning.

16. **(A)** Earth, and Venus are similar in size, according to images taken by satellites.
    (B) Earth is similar in size to Venus, according to images taken by satellites.
    (C) Earth and Venus are similar in size, according to images taken by satellites.

17. **(A)** Either flowers, candy or cards are usually given to loved ones on Valentine's Day.
    (B) Either flowers, candy, or cards are usually given to loved ones on Valentine's Day.
    (C) Either flowers candy, or cards are usually given to loved ones on Valentine's Day.

18. **(A)** A jury debates and determines the verdict in some court cases.
    (B) A jury debates, and determines the verdict in some court cases.
    (C) A jury debates, and determines, the verdict in some court cases.

Unit 3
Building Sentences

19. **(A)** The race car smoked, sputtered and stalled before it was able to cross the finish line.
(B) The sputtering race car smoked, and stalled before it was able to cross the finish line.
(C) The race care smoked, sputtered, and stalled before it was able to cross the finish line.

---

20. **(A)** Deep sea divers exploring ancient shipwrecks uncovered valuable treasures there.
(B) Deep sea divers have explored ancient shipwrecks and uncovered valuable treasures there.
(C) Deep sea divers have explored ancient shipwrecks, and uncovered ancient shipwrecks there.

---

21. **(A)** Either Mrs. Caspan, Mr. Johnson, or the principal will speak at the assembly today.
(B) Either Mrs. Caspan Mr. Johnson or the principal, will speak at the assembly today.
(C) Either Mrs. Caspan, Mr. Johnson or the principal will speak at the assembly today.

---

22. **(A)** The squid, cuttlefish share some of the same physical characteristics and octopus.
(B) The squid, cuttlefish and the octopus, share some of the same physical characteristics.
(C) The squid, cuttlefish, and octopus share some of the same physical characteristics.

---

23. **(A)** A hurricane can have devastating effects or a blizzard or a tornado on a community.
(B) A hurricane blizzard, or a tornado can have devastating effects on a community.
(C) A hurricane, a blizzard, or a tornado can have devastating effects on a community.

---

24. **(A)** Enrique planted the flowers, but forgot he had to water them.
(B) Enrique planted the flowers but forgot he had to water them.
(C) Enrique bought but planted the flowers and forgot he had to water them.

---

25. **(A)** The committee reads, answers all the group members' questions.
(B) The committee reads and answers all the group members' questions.
(C) The committee reads, and answers, all the group members' questions.

---

26. **(A)** Minya wrote a poem, but decided to revise it.
(B) Minya wrote a poem decided to revise it.
(C) Minya wrote a poem but decided to revise it.

Unit 4
Building Sentences

You can build one sentence that contains two different but related sentences to express an idea. This is known as a **compound sentence** and is formed when two or more simple sentences are joined by either a comma and a conjunction, such as *and, but,* or *or,* or by a semicolon (;). When you join two sentences with a semicolon, do *not* use a conjunction with it.

Many fish tumble over the falls**, but** most survive the drop.

Annie Taylor inspired other daredevils**;** she went over the falls in a barrel in 1901.

Niagara Falls

Choose the words to correctly build a compound sentence.

1. Niagara Falls is a city in New York
   (A) and it's a city in Canada.
   (B) , and it's a city in Canada.
   (C) ; and it's a city in Canada.

2. Tourist travel to the falls began in the 1820s
   (A) ; and within fifty years, it became the area's top tourist spot.
   (B) ; within fifty years, it became the area's top tourist spot.
   (C) and within fifty years it became the area's top tourist spot.

3. The falls are a tourist attraction
   (A) , but they also provide electric power.
   (B) ; but they also provide electric power.
   (C) they also provide electric power.

4. Visitors may stroll next to the falls on the Whitewater Boardwalk
   (A) , or they may take a boat ride on Maid of the Mist.
   (B) or they may take a boat ride on Maid of the Mist.
   (C) ; or they may take a boat ride on Maid of the Mist.

5. An ice jam once blocked the falls
   (A) and the roaring waters slowed to a trickle.
   (B) the roaring waters slowed to a trickle.
   (C) , and the roaring waters slowed to a trickle.

6. The Horseshoe Falls lie on the Canadian side
   (A) and the American Falls are in New York.
   (B) ; the American Falls are in New York.
   (C) , the American Falls are in New York.

Unit 4
Building Sentences

The Night Life

7. The moon doesn't really change shape
   (A) , but what we see of it changes.
   (B) ; but what we see of it changes.
   (C) what we see of it changes.

---

8. Nocturnal animals become active at night
   (A) , they rest during the day.
   (B) they rest during the day.
   (C) , and they rest during the day.

---

9. An *aurora,* a band of light in the sky, might be arched like a rainbow
   (A) , or it could have a more random shape.
   (B) ; or it could have a more random shape.
   (C) or it could have a more random shape.

---

10. Moonflowers bloom in the evening
    (A) ; and they close when the sun comes up.
    (B) , and they close when the sun comes up.
    (C) and they close when the sun comes up.

---

11. Meteor showers are a delight to sky watchers
    (A) clouds can spoil the view.
    (B) , but clouds can spoil the view.
    (C) but clouds can spoil the view.

---

12. City lights are often reflected by clouds
    (A) , and the sky appears to glow.
    (B) ; and the sky appears to glow.
    (C) , the sky appears to glow.

---

13. Jupiter has twenty-eight moons
    (A) , four of them can be seen with binoculars at night.
    (B) ; and four of them can be seen with binoculars at night.
    (C) ; four of them can be seen with binoculars at night.

---

14. Is that the chirping of a cricket
    (A) or is it a katydid that I hear?
    (B) , or is it a katydid that I hear?
    (C) ; or is it a katydid that I hear?

Unit 4
Building Sentences

You might need to include information in your writing that cannot stand alone as its own sentence. In this case, you can build a **complex sentence,** which is made of one independent clause and one or more dependent clauses.

- An **independent clause** can stand alone as a sentence.

  You should always wear a helmet.
- A **dependent clause** has a subject and a verb but cannot stand alone and begins with a subordinating conjunction such as *after, because, if, since, until,* and *when*.

  You should always wear a helmet **when you ride your bike**.
- If a dependent clause appears at the beginning of a complex sentence, use a comma after it.

  Even though many people try, you can't please everyone.
- Do not use a comma before a dependent clause that follows an independent clause unless the clause is *not* necessary to the meaning of the sentence.

  Most of you know **that I am running for class president**.

  I am prepared for the debate, which will take place in the gym.

Choose the words that correctly build a complex sentence.

15. _____ he saved the lion's life.
    (A) Although the mouse was very small,
    (B) The ropes were thick
    (C) The mouse was very small

16. The milkmaid's mother said, "Don't count your chickens _____."
    (A) they will hatch
    (B) before they are hatched
    (C) you might be disappointed

17. The ant had a lot of food, _____.
    (A) which he appreciated when winter came
    (B) he worked hard
    (C) he enjoyed every meal

18. _____ he decided they were sour.
    (A) The fox had many failed attempts
    (B) Since the fox couldn't reach the grapes,
    (C) The grapes were hanging on the vine

19. The mice devised a plan _____.
    (A) they wanted to make their home safe again
    (B) they put a bell around the cat's neck
    (C) that they were afraid to carry out

Unit 4
Building Sentences

20. The tortoise crossed the finish line ____.
(A) he was huffing and puffing
(B) the hare was asleep
(C) while the hare was still napping

21. ____ that appearances can be deceiving.
(A) A wolf in sheep's clothing shows
(B) As though some trouble could be nearby
(C) Be cautious at all times

22. ____ honesty is the best policy.
(A) In every case,
(B) Remember this lesson
(C) As the greedy woodsman learned,

23. You can avoid falling in a well ____.
(A) before watching your step
(B) if you look before you leap
(C) like the goat did

24. The fox didn't realize how much misery loves company ____.
(A) until he lost his tail
(B) he was caught in a trap
(C) he tried to convince the others

25. ____ do it with all your strength.
(A) He touched it gently
(B) Whatever you do,
(C) The boy touched the prickly plant

26. The hunter's story should teach you ____.
(A) which was a good lesson
(B) he was following a lion's tracks
(C) that a hero is brave in deeds as well as words

27. Although the two frogs needed a new home, ____.
(A) one of them was wise enough to think about the consequences of making their home in a deep well
(B) as though they couldn't find another one
(C) in order to find another pond

Unit 4

Building Sentences

You can also build a **compound-complex sentence** when there is a lot of information to include in a sentence, some of which cannot stand alone. A compound-complex sentence contains two or more independent clauses and at least one dependent clause.

INDEPENDENT CLAUSE

Natural resources are found in the environment, and
they often provide materials **that help people improve their lives**.

INDEPENDENT CLAUSE DEPENDENT CLAUSE

- Don't forget that a dependent clause cannot stand alone even though it may have a subject and a verb.

Natural Resources

Which group of words can be added to build a compound-complex sentence?

28. _____ a particular resource might become more valuable, or it might lose value.
    (A) Because of technology,
    (B) As new uses are discovered,
    (C) Through the years,

29. People have used trees throughout history, and this natural resource is especially beneficial _____.
    (A) to lumber companies
    (B) such as building homes and furniture
    (C) because it can be replaced

30. Metals and minerals cannot be replaced _____ and that is why they're called *nonrenewable resources*.
    (A) once they are taken from the earth,
    (B) for millions of years,
    (C) or created,

31. Pesticides improve crops, _____ if rivers become polluted.
    (A) but they can kill animals
    (B) which doesn't matter
    (C) but cause harm

32. Humans consume a lot of coal and oil, but they'll have to use other sources of energy _____.
    (A) when these fossil fuels are gone
    (B) before long
    (C) such as solar power

Unit 4

Building Sentences

33. Deserts of the world are growing bigger, _____ where essential crops are grown.

(A) just like the land
(B) and they are taking over farmland
(C) spreading sand on places

34. _____ hot water runs under the ground, and it is piped up to heat homes and factories.

(A) Throughout Iceland, surprisingly,
(B) In modern times,
(C) Although Iceland is quite cold,

35. People across the world have a variety of skills _____ and these are also natural resources.

(A) learned from experience
(B) that they can apply,
(C) and useful talents,

36. We cannot always renew natural resources _____ so we should remember to use them wisely.

(A) after they have been depleted,
(B) that are gone,
(C) very easily,

37. _____ people could walk to places instead of driving, or they could use public transportation.

(A) In the morning,
(B) Unless a car is absolutely necessary,
(C) On sunny days,

38. This would help to reduce air pollution caused by car exhaust, and it would help to save oil _____.

(A) because fewer people would be driving
(B) in the long run
(C) all over the United States

The First LAP
Language Activity Pages

A. Exercising Your Skill

You have been learning how to build different types of sentences. Choose the term that correctly completes each of the statements below.

1. To build a sentence, you must have a _____ and a simple predicate.
   (A) conjunction **(B)** subject **(C)** dependent clause
2. A _____ is two or more simple predicates connected by a conjunction.
   (A) compound predicate **(B)** simple predicate **(C)** compound sentence
3. To make a compound subject, you must connect two _____ with a conjunction.
   (A) simple subjects **(B)** simple sentences **(C)** simple predicates
4. To build a _____ sentence, you must have two or more independent clauses and at least one dependent clause.
   (A) compound **(B)** complex **(C)** compound-complex
5. To build a _____ sentence, you must have one independent clause and at least one dependent clause.
   (A) compound **(B)** complex **(C)** compound-complex

B. Expanding Your Skill

Read the clauses below. Follow the directions, and choose words from the right column to build sentences correctly. **DC** means add a dependent clause, and **IC** means add an independent clause.

1. Although she had set her alarm clock, (IC)	**(A)** even though she had to hurry.
2. Ming Na had to gulp down her breakfast (DC)	**(B)** as she looked out the window.
3. The bus was turning the corner (DC)	**(C)** because she was running late.
4. After she found her backpack, (IC)	**(D)** Ming Na still overslept.
5. Ming Na put on her jacket and a hat (DC)	**(E)** she threw it over her shoulder.
6. Because it was cold outside this morning, (IC)	**(F)** Ming Na also put on a scarf.
7. She surprisingly made it to school on time (DC)	**(G)** before she left.
8. (IC) as though she was the only one who ever overslept.	**(H)** Everyone looked at her

C. Exploring Language

Narrative Writing Read the story below. Then number your paper from 1 to 5. Choose the dependent clauses from the box to complete each sentence.

(A) how he would spend the extra time.
(B) although his mother had told him repeatedly to go to bed.
(C) until he woke up several hours later,
(D) which was where he always liked to sit.
(E) When he heard the rumbling of the bus,

Antoine was dozing off as he waited at the bus stop. (1) _____ he stood up from the bench and got in line. Antoine had stayed up late the night before, (2) _____ He would be fine, he told himself. Now Antoine settled into a seat at the back of the bus, (3) _____ Antoine was thinking he'd probably stay up late more often, and he considered (4) _____ Antoine felt pretty good about his decision (5) _____ drooling on the back seat of the quiet, empty bus.

D. Expressing Yourself

Choose one of these activities. When you are finished, give your paper to your teacher.

1. Read through a textbook, and try to find at least one example each of a compound sentence, a complex sentence, and a compound-complex sentence. Write the sentences on your paper, and underline the dependent clauses. Which type of sentence appears most often? Which type appears the least?

2. WORK with a PARTNER Play a "complex sentence" game with a partner. One partner writes an independent clause while the other partner adds a dependent clause. Take turns going first. After you have written three sentences, share them with another pair of partners, and read the sentences that they wrote.

Unit 5
Combining Sentences

Combining with Subjects and Predicates

Writers sometimes combine short, related sentences to make them sound better and to avoid repetition. One way to do this is to combine subjects or predicates.

- Use *and, or,* or *either/or* to combine subjects and create a compound subject.

  The computer needs to be fixed. The printer needs to be fixed.

  The computer and the printer need to be fixed.

  Team A will go first. Team B will go first.

  Either Team A or Team B will go first.

- Use *and, but,* or *or* to combine predicates and create a compound predicate.

  Animals communicate. They make sounds. Animals cannot talk.

  Animals **communicate and make sounds but cannot talk.**

When you combine sentences, make sure the new sentence is not too long, even if it makes sense.

Everyday Tools

What is the best way to combine the following sentences?

1. A blender purees vegetables. A blender chops ice.
   (A) A blender purees vegetables, and it also chops ice.
   (B) A blender purees vegetables, and a blender chops ice.
   (C) A blender purees vegetables and chops ice.

2. A ladder helps people reach higher places. A stool helps people reach higher places.
   (A) A ladder or a stool helps people reach higher places.
   (B) A ladder helps people reach higher places, or a stool helps people reach higher places.
   (C) A ladder helps people reach higher places, or a stool does too.

3. A stopwatch measures time. A sundial measures time. A metronome measures time.
   (A) A stopwatch measures time, and so do a sundial and a metronome.
   (B) A stopwatch measures time, a sundial measures time, and a metronome measures time.
   (C) A stopwatch, a sundial, and a metronome measure time.

Unit 5
Combining Sentences

When simple subjects have been combined, the verb must agree in number with the new compound subject.

- When the subjects are joined by *and,* use the plural form of the verb most of the time.

  Mom, Dad, and I **cook** dinner together. (*not* cooks)

- When the subjects are joined by *or,* the verb should agree with the nearest subject.

  Shonda or her brothers **deliver** the newspapers. (*not* delivers)

What is the best way to combine the following sentences?

4. Pencils help us express our thoughts to others. Pens help us express our thoughts to others.
   (A) Pencils and pens help us express our thoughts to others.
   (B) Pencils and pens helps us express our thoughts to others.
   (C) Pencils help us and pens help us express our thoughts to others.

5. Sunglasses protect you from the sun. An umbrella protects you from the sun.
   (A) Sunglasses protect you from the sun, or an umbrella protects you too.
   (B) Sunglasses or an umbrella protect you from the sun.
   (C) Sunglasses or an umbrella protects you from the sun.

6. A flashlight is helpful when the lights go out. Candles are helpful when the lights go out.
   (A) A flashlight is helpful when the lights go out, and candles are helpful when the lights go out.
   (B) A flashlight and candles are helpful when the lights go out.
   (C) A flashlight is helpful when the lights go out, and candles are too.

7. One large suitcase holds my clothes. A backpack holds my clothes.
   (A) One large suitcase holds my clothes, and a backpack holds my clothes.
   (B) One large suitcase and a backpack hold my clothes.
   (C) One large suitcase and a backpack holds my clothes.

8. The silverware belongs in that drawer. The measuring cups belong in that drawer. The serving spoons belong in that drawer.
   (A) The silverware, the measuring cups, and the serving spoons belong in that drawer.
   (B) The silverware belongs in that drawer and so do the measuring cups and the serving spoons.
   (C) The silverware belongs in that drawer, and the measuring cups belong in that drawer, and the serving spoons belong in that drawer.

Unit 5
Combining Sentences

Combining with Adjectives

When combining sentences, look for adjectives that can be moved and placed in front of the nouns they describe. In the newly combined sentence, make sure each adjective describes the correct noun.

The temples rise toward the sky. The temples are **ancient**.

Incorrect: The temples rise toward the **ancient** sky.

Correct: The **ancient** temples rise toward the sky.

Sometimes adjectives can be joined with *and* and placed after the noun.

The temples are tall. The temples are ancient.

The temples are **tall and ancient**.

Remember that the goal of combining sentences is to create one clearer, shorter sentence.

A Glimpse at Greatness

What is the best way to combine the following sentences?

9. Taharqo was a king who ruled for twenty-seven years. He was a famous king. He was Nubian.
   (A) Taharqo was a Nubian king who ruled for twenty-seven famous years.
   (B) Taharqo was a famous Nubian king who ruled for twenty-seven years.
   (C) Taharqo was a famous king, and he was a Nubian who ruled for twenty-seven years.

10. Jewelry survives from the Nubian kingdom. It was handcrafted. The jewelry is gold.
   (A) Jewelry that is gold and that is handcrafted survives from the Nubian kingdom.
   (B) Handcrafted jewelry survives from the gold Nubian kingdom.
   (C) Handcrafted gold jewelry survives from the Nubian kingdom.

11. Adventurers robbed some Nubian temples. The adventurers were greedy.
   (A) Adventurers robbed some greedy Nubian temples.
   (B) Adventurers who were greedy robbed some Nubian temples.
   (C) Greedy adventurers robbed some Nubian temples.

12. The pyramids are now mounds of stone. The pyramids are destroyed. The mounds are shapeless.
   (A) The destroyed pyramids are now shapeless mounds of stone.
   (B) The pyramids that are destroyed are now mounds of stone, and they are shapeless.
   (C) The pyramids are destroyed, and the pyramids are also mounds of shapeless stone.

Unit 5

Combining Sentences

Combining with Adverbs

Look for adverbs that modify the same action when you want to combine sentences. Make sure the adverb is placed correctly in the combined sentence. Although adverbs can often be placed in different places within a sentence, it should be clear which word the adverb is describing.

The band played their songs. They played them **loudly**. They played them **fast**.

Incorrect: The **loudly** band played their songs **fast**.

Correct: The band played their songs **loudly** and **fast**.

Animal Motion

What is the best way to combine the following sentences?

13. A cheetah runs. It runs fastest of all animals at about seventy miles per hour.
   (A) A cheetah runs, and it runs fastest of all animals at about seventy miles per hour.
   (B) A cheetah runs fastest, and it is fastest of all animals at about seventy miles per hour.
   (C) A cheetah runs fastest of all animals at about seventy miles per hour.

---

14. A turtle plods along down a deserted road. It moves lazily.
   (A) A turtle lazily plods along down a deserted road.
   (B) A turtle plods along down a deserted road, and it plods lazily.
   (C) A turtle plods along down a lazily deserted road.

---

15. Deer meet at the pond to drink water. They meet there daily.
   (A) Deer meet at the daily pond to drink water.
   (B) Deer meet at the pond to drink water, and they do it daily.
   (C) Deer meet daily at the pond to drink water.

---

16. The lion creeps up on the impala. The lion creeps up quietly.
   (A) The lion creeps up on the impala, and it creeps quietly too.
   (B) The lion quietly creeps up on the impala.
   (C) The quietly lion creeps up on the impala.

---

17. A herd of swans swims across the lake. The swans swim gracefully.
   (A) A herd of swans swims gracefully across the lake.
   (B) A herd of swans swims across the gracefully lake.
   (C) A herd of swans swims across the lake, and the swans swim gracefully.

Unit 5

Combining Sentences

Try different ways to combine sentences when you write. Look for subjects and predicates that can be combined to form compound subjects and compound predicates. Also look for adjectives that describe the same noun and adverbs that modify the same action in related sentences. Always reread the newly combined sentence to make sure it makes sense.

What is the best way to combine the following sentences?

18. Maps help people find their way. A compass helps people find their way.
   (A) Maps or a compass helps people find their way.
   (B) Maps help people, or a compass helps people find their way.
   (C) Maps help people find their way or a compass.

---

19. Our family talks at the reunion. Our family eats at the reunion.
   (A) Our family talks at the reunion, and they eat too.
   (B) Our family talks and eats at the reunion.
   (C) Our family talks, and our family eats at the reunion.

---

20. The crowd jumped during the game. The crowd cheered. They did it loudly.
   (A) The crowd jumped and cheered during the game, and they did it loudly.
   (B) The crowed jumped and cheered loudly during the game.
   (C) The crowd loudly jumped, and the crowd cheered during the game.

---

21. Tyra writes in her journal. She writes in her journal every night before she goes to sleep.
   (A) Tyra writes in her journal, and she writes in her journal every night before she goes to sleep.
   (B) Tyra writes in her journal before she every night goes to sleep.
   (C) Tyra writes in her journal every night before she goes to sleep.

---

22. An army of frogs jumped into the water. The frogs were frightened. They jumped quickly.
   (A) An army of frogs that were frightened jumped into the water, and they jumped quickly.
   (B) An army of frogs jumped, and they jumped into the frightened water quickly.
   (C) An army of frightened frogs quickly jumped into the water.

---

23. Did Patrick bring these cookies? Did Rachel bring these cookies? The cookies are delicious.
   (A) Did Patrick or Rachel bring these delicious cookies?
   (B) Did Patrick or did Rachel bring these cookies that are delicious?
   (C) Did Patrick bring these delicious cookies, or did Rachel bring them?

Unit 5
Combining Sentences

24. Craig picked up the box. Craig needed help carrying the box. The box is huge.
   (A) Craig picked up the box, but Craig needed help carrying the box that is huge.
   (B) Craig picked up the huge box but needed help carrying it.
   (C) Craig picked up the huge box, but Craig needed help carrying the huge box.

25. A crane raises objects. A crane lowers objects. The objects are heavy.
   (A) A crane raises or lowers heavy objects.
   (B) A crane raises or a crane lowers objects that are heavy.
   (C) A heavy crane raises or lowers objects.

26. A snake swallows its food. It swallows it whole. Its food is unchewed.
   (A) A whole snake swallows its unchewed food.
   (B) A snake swallows its food, and it swallows it unchewed and whole.
   (C) A snake swallows its unchewed food whole.

27. Emily doesn't want to see that movie. Emilio doesn't want to see that movie.
   (A) Neither Emily wants to see that movie nor does Emilio.
   (B) Neither Emily nor Emilio wants to see that movie.
   (C) Emily doesn't want to see that movie nor does Emilio.

28. Lemonade tastes great. Iced tea tastes great. Either one tastes great on a hot day.
   (A) Lemonade tastes great, or iced tea tastes great on a hot day.
   (B) Lemonade or iced tea tastes great, and either one tastes great on a hot day.
   (C) Either lemonade or iced tea tastes great on a hot day.

29. Guitars must be tuned. Violins must be tuned. They must be tuned carefully.
   (A) Guitars and violins must be tuned carefully.
   (B) Guitars and violins must be tuned, and they must be tuned carefully.
   (C) Guitars must be tuned, and violins must be tuned carefully.

30. Peel the banana before you put it in your cereal. Cut the banana before you put it in your cereal.
   (A) Peel the banana, and cut the banana before you put it in your cereal.
   (B) Peel and cut the banana before you put it in your cereal.
   (C) Peel the banana before you put it in your cereal, and cut it.

Unit 6
Combining Sentences

Combining with Prepositional Phrases

Prepositional phrases that refer to the same word in related sentences can be combined. In the newly combined sentence, it should be clear to what or to whom the phrases refer.

Pioneers traveled across the country. Pioneers traveled in covered wagons.

Pioneers traveled **in covered wagons across the country**.

- If the combined prepositional phrases are showing time order, it is sometimes necessary to join them with *and*.

The ball rolled across the table. It rolled into the hole.

The ball rolled **across the table and into the hole**.

What is the best way to combine the following sentences?

1. The piano recital is in the auditorium. The piano recital is at my school.
   (A) The piano recital is in the auditorium, and it is at my school.
   (B) The piano recital is in the auditorium at my school.
   (C) The piano recital is in the auditorium, and the auditorium is at my school.

2. The space shuttle soared, through the air. It soared beyond the clouds.
   (A) The space shuttle soared, and through the air, and beyond the clouds.
   (B) The space shuttle soared through the air, and the space shuttle soared beyond the clouds.
   (C) The space shuttle soared through the air and beyond the clouds.

3. The octopus hides in dark places. The octopus hides at the bottom of the sea.
   (A) The octopus hides in darks places, and it hides at the bottom of the sea.
   (B) The octopus hides in dark places at the bottom of the sea.
   (C) The octopus hides in dark places and hides at the bottom of the sea.

4. Record the reading on the spring scale. Record it in your learning log.
   (A) Record the reading on the spring scale, and record it in your learning log.
   (B) Record the reading on the spring scale, and record the reading in your learning log.
   (C) Record the reading on the spring scale in your learning log.

5. Rosa Parks sat firmly in her seat. She sat on a bus. She was in Montgomery, Alabama.
   (A) Rosa Parks sat firmly in her seat, and she sat on a bus in Montgomery, Alabama.
   (B) Rosa Parks sat firmly in her seat, and she sat on a bus, and she was in Montgomery, Alabama.
   (C) Rosa Parks sat firmly in her seat on a bus in Montgomery, Alabama.

Unit 6
Combining Sentences

Combining with Appositives and Appositive Phrases

- An **appositive** is a noun that is placed next to another noun to identify it or add information about it. An **appositive phrase** includes an appositive and any words that modify it. Closely related sentences may contain information that can be combined into one sentence by using an appositive or an appositive phrase. The appositive or appositive phrase should modify the correct noun in the new sentence.

  Gary Soto grew up in Fresno, California. He is my favorite writer.

  Gary Soto**, my favorite writer,** grew up in Fresno, California.

- Use commas to set off the appositive unless the sentence would be vague without the appositive.

  His novel was published in 2000. It is entitled *Nickel and Dime*.

  His novel ***Nickel and Dime*** was published in 2000. (no commas needed because the sentence would be vague without the appositive *Nickel and Dime*)

What is the best way to combine the following sentences?

6. Argentina's capital is one of the largest cities in South America. Argentina's capital is Buenos Aires.
   (A) Argentina's capital, Buenos Aires, is one of the largest cities in South America.
   (B) Buenos Aires is Argentina's capital, and it is one of the largest cities in South America.
   (C) Argentina's capital is one of the largest cities in South America, and Buenos Aires is Argentina's capital.

---

7. Some Native Americans live in pueblos just as their ancestors did. Pueblos are villages with clusters of apartments.
   (A) Some Native Americans still live in pueblos, and pueblos are villages with clusters of apartments.
   (B) Some Native Americans, villages with clusters of apartments, still live in pueblos just as their ancestors did.
   (C) Some Native Americans still live in pueblos, villages with clusters of apartments, just as their ancestors did.

---

8. Borscht is a popular meal in Russia. It is a soup made from beets.
   (A) Borscht, a soup made from beets, is a popular meal in Russia.
   (B) Borscht is a popular meal in Russia, a soup made from beets.
   (C) Borscht is a popular meal in Russia, and it is a soup made from beets.

Unit 6

Combining Sentences

Combining with Participles and Participial Phrases

- A **participle** is a verb form that can act as an adjective to describe a noun or a pronoun. A participle is often formed by adding *-d*, *-ed*, or *-ing* to a verb. Like adjectives, participles from related sentences can be moved and placed in front of the nouns they describe in the newly combined sentence.

  The Asian elephant needs protection. The Asian elephant is endangered.

  The **endangered** Asian elephant needs protection.

- A **participial phrase** includes the participle and any other words that complete its meaning. You may be able to combine two related sentences by using the verb from one of the sentences to create a participial phrase. The participial phrase must be placed next to the noun it describes.

  The elephant prepares for a refreshing shower. The elephant fills its trunk with water.

  Preparing for a refreshing shower, the elephant fills its trunk with water.

What is the best way to combine the following sentences?

9. The soccer team was encouraged by their victory. They were ready to play again.
   (A) Encouraged by their victory, the soccer team was ready to play again.
   (B) The soccer team was encouraged by their victory, and they were ready to play again.
   (C) The soccer team was ready to play again encouraged by their victory.

10. Cats use a paw to clean behind their ears. They moisten the paw.
   (A) Cats use a moistened paw to clean behind their ears.
   (B) Cats use a paw to clean behind their moistened ears.
   (C) Cats use a paw that they have moistened to clean behind their ears.

11. My sister was the only one who could calm down the baby. The baby was crying.
   (A) My crying sister was the only one who could calm down the baby.
   (B) My sister was the only one who could calm down the crying baby.
   (C) My sister was the only one who could calm down the baby, and the baby was crying.

12. Erik dreams of fame. He sits at the piano.
   (A) Erik, dreaming of fame, sits at the piano.
   (B) Erik dreams of fame, and he sits at the piano.
   (C) Erik dreams of fame, and he is sitting at the piano.

Unit 6

Combining Sentences

Combining to Make Compound or Complex Sentences

Sentences that contain related information can often be combined to form compound or complex sentences.

- There are two ways to form a **compound sentence.** One way is to use a comma and a conjunction such as *and, but,* or *or* to join the sentences. Another way is to use a semicolon to join the sentences. When you use a semicolon, you should *not* use a conjunction.

  An antibiotic fights bacteria. It is not effective against viruses.

  An antibiotic fights bacteria**, but** it is not effective against viruses.

  An antibiotic fights bacteria**;** it is not effective against viruses.

- To form a **complex sentence,** join the clauses with a subordinating conjunction, such as *after, although, as, because, if, since, that, until,* and *when*. Consider the meaning of each subordinating conjunction before you use it.

  We wanted an Irish wolfhound. We saw how big they get!

  We wanted an Irish wolfhound **until** we saw how big they get!

What is the correct way to combine each pair of sentences to form a compound or complex sentence?

13. Medicine can be swallowed. It can be injected into the body.

(A) Medicine can be swallowed it can be injected into the body.
(B) Medicine can be swallowed and it can be injected into the body.
(C) Medicine can be swallowed, or it can be injected into the body.

---

14. Penicillin is an important medical discovery. It kills bacteria.

(A) After penicillin kills bacteria, it is an important medical discovery.
(B) Because penicillin kills bacteria, it is an important medical discovery.
(C) Penicillin is an important medical discovery it kills bacteria.

---

15. Asthma medicine is inhaled. It goes directly to the lungs.

(A) When asthma medicine is inhaled, it goes directly to the lungs.
(B) Although asthma medicine is inhaled; it goes directly to the lungs.
(C) Asthma medicine is inhaled, it goes directly to the lungs.

---

16. A doctor must prescribe some medicines. Others are available "over the counter."

(A) A doctor must prescribe some medicines; but others are available "over the counter."
(B) A doctor must prescribe some medicines, others are available "over the counter."
(C) A doctor must prescribe some medicines; others are available "over the counter."

Unit 6
Combining Sentences

When you write, keep in mind all of the strategies you have learned for combining sentences. Look for ways to combine sentences using prepositional phrases, appositives and appositive phrases, and participles and participial phrases. Also consider forming compound or complex sentences.

Gone to the Dogs

Choose the correct and best way to combine the following sentences.

17. The beagle is a good tracking dog. It has an excellent sense of smell.
   (A) The beagle is a good tracking dog because it has an excellent sense of smell.
   (B) Unless it has an excellent sense of smell, the beagle is a good tracking dog.
   (C) When the beagle is a good tracking dog, it has an excellent sense of smell.

18. My puppy's bed is on the floor. The bed is in my room.
   (A) My puppy's bed is on the floor, and the bed is in my room.
   (B) My puppy's bed is on the floor, in my room.
   (C) My puppy's bed is on the floor in my room.

19. The dog's tail means that it is excited. The tail is wagging.
   (A) The dog's wagging tail means that it is excited.
   (B) The dog's tail that is wagging means that it is excited.
   (C) The wagging dog's tail means that it is excited.

20. Domestic dogs are descendants of the wolf. Huskies and greyhounds are domestic dogs.
   (A) Domestic dogs are descendants of the wolf, and huskies and greyhounds are domestic dogs.
   (B) Domestic dogs, such as huskies and greyhounds, are descendants of the wolf.
   (C) Domestic dogs are descendants of the wolf, such as huskies and greyhounds.

21. Humans tamed dogs about 12,000 years ago. The animals have been great companions.
   (A) Humans tamed dogs about 12,000 years ago; and the animals have been great companions.
   (B) Because the animals have been great companions, humans tamed dogs about 12,000 years ago.
   (C) Since humans tamed dogs about 12,000 years ago, the animals have been great companions.

Unit 6

Combining Sentences

Wolves

22. A wolf is a hunter. A wolf is strong. It can pull down prey ten times its own weight.

(A) A wolf is a hunter and is strong; it can pull down prey ten times its own weight.

(B) A wolf is a hunter that is also strong and can pull down prey ten times its own weight.

(C) A wolf is a strong hunter that can pull down prey ten times its own weight.

---

23. Wolves can communicate with each other over long distances. They do this by howling.

(A) Wolves that are howling can communicate with each other over long distances.

(B) Howling wolves can communicate with each other over long distances.

(C) Wolves can communicate with each other over long, howling distances.

---

24. Some scientists study the howling of wolves. They study them in the wild. They wonder what the wolf is trying to communicate.

(A) Because some scientists wonder what the wolf is trying to communicate, they study the howling of wolves in the wild.

(B) Some scientists study the howling of wolves, and they do so in the wild; and they wonder what the wolf is trying to communicate.

(C) Because some scientists study them in the wild, scientists wonder what the wolf is trying to communicate, and some scientists study the howling of wolves.

---

25. The gray wolf is one of the most common kinds of wolves. It lives in the United States. The gray wolf is also known as the tundra wolf.

(A) The gray wolf is one of the most common kinds of wolves known as the tundra wolf, and it lives in the United States.

(B) Living in the United States, the gray wolf is one of the most common kinds of wolves, and it is known as the tundra wolf too.

(C) Also known as the tundra wolf, the gray wolf is one of the most common kinds of wolves living in the United States.

---

26. The wolf didn't know what to do when the farmer chased it off his land. The wolf was confused. It was only trying to find food for its pups.

(A) Because it was only trying to find food for its pups, the wolf didn't know what to do when the farmer chased it off his land, and the wolf was confused.

(B) The confused wolf didn't know what to do when the farmer chased it off his land; it was only trying to find food for its pups.

(C) The wolf that was confused didn't know what to do when the farmer chased it off his land, or it was only trying to find food for its pups.

The Second LAP
Language Activity Pages

A. Exercising Your Skill

You have been learning about different ways to combine sentences. Answer these questions about what you have learned.

1. How has the writer combined the following sentences?
   I spotted some Canada geese in the park. They were near the lake.
   I spotted some Canada geese in the park near the lake.
   (A) Adjectives have been moved in front of nouns.
   (B) Prepositional phrases have been combined.
   (C) An appositive has been formed.

2. How has the writer combined the following sentences?
   Canada geese have large bodies. Their bodies are brownish-gray.
   Canada geese have large brownish-gray bodies.
   (A) Adjectives have been moved in front of nouns.
   (B) Prepositional phrases have been combined.
   (C) A participle has been formed.

3. How has the writer combined the following sentences?
   They can be aggressive birds. They are also quick to make friends.
   Although they can be aggressive birds, they are also quick to make friends.
   (A) A complex sentence has been formed.
   (B) Adverbs have been moved.
   (C) A compound sentence has been formed.

B. Expanding Your Skill

Which is the best way to combine the following sentences?

1. John looked at the painting. He didn't understand it. The painting was abstract.
   (A) John looked at the abstract painting but didn't understand it.
   (B) John looked at the painting but didn't understand it; the painting was abstract.
   (C) Looking at the painting, John didn't understand it, and it was abstract.

2. Beth ran to the door when she heard a knock. Beth ran quickly. She was expecting a package.
   (A) Because Beth was expecting a package, she ran quickly to the door when she heard a knock.
   (B) Beth ran and she ran quickly to the door when she heard a knock because she was expecting a package.
   (C) Beth ran to the door when she heard a knock, and she ran quickly because she was expecting a package.

C. Exploring Language

Expository Writing Read the following story. Then number your paper from 1 to 5. Choose the participial or appositive phrase from the box that best completes each sentence.

(A) Impressed by Bly's writing skills,
(B) Pretending to be insane,
(C) a pioneer in journalism,
(D) depictions of living and working conditions of the poor,
(E) the *Pittsburgh Dispatch*,

Nellie Bly, (1) _____ was one of the first investigative reporters. Bly began writing for a newspaper, (2) _____ after she wrote an angry letter to the editor. (3) _____ the editor contacted Bly and offered her a job. From her first articles, (4) _____ Bly was recognized for her integrity, compassion, and commitment to social reform. (5) _____ Bly once got herself admitted to a mental hospital so she could observe firsthand how the patients were treated.

D. Expressing Yourself

Choose one of these activities. When you are finished, give your paper to your teacher.

1. WORK with a PARTNER Choose a topic or a period in history that both you and your partner are interested in. Do some research on the Internet, in an encyclopedia, or in another source to find some information about it. Take notes as you conduct your research. Then combine different parts of your notes, especially sentences, to make new sentences.

2. Write a newspaper article about a change you would like to see made in your community or at your school. Add participial and appositive phrases to your sentences to add more details or to help explain or describe something. Also combine any short sentences when possible.

Unit 7

The Sound of Language

Writers often use certain words because of the way they sound. This can make their sentences more interesting to read and more fun to write. There are many techniques that use the sound of language. One of these techniques is rhyme. You would be most likely to use rhyme in poetry.

- One type of rhyme is called **internal rhyme,** which means that two or more words within a line rhyme.

  Snowing and **blowing**, the blizzard keeps **growing**!

Rhyme Time!

Which sentence has internal rhyme?

1. **(A)** No matter how hard I try, I'll sit here all day.
   (B) It doesn't matter how hard I try; I'll have to sit here all day.
   (C) Try as I may, I'll sit here all day.

2. **(A)** I sit at this table because I cannot eat one more bite.
   (B) I have to sit here until I clean my plate.
   (C) I won't leave the table until I am ready and able.

3. **(A)** My brother says, "Just grin and bear it; you can eat that last carrot!"
   (B) My brother says, "It's not that big of a deal; just eat it!"
   (C) My brother says to eat it and smile.

4. **(A)** I wish my fork were the mouth of some kind of animal.
   (B) Oh, if only my fork were the beak of a stork.
   (C) If I could, I'd give this food to someone who wants it.

5. **(A)** I'd give my carrot to the stork because I am too full to eat it.
   (B) My carrot I would feed it because I surely don't need it.
   (C) I would shovel this food into that bird's big belly.

6. **(A)** That would be nice, but storks don't eat carrots.
   (B) Nice try, but storks eat fish; they don't eat vegetables.
   (C) Storks don't eat carrots—nice wish—but they sure do like fish.

7. **(A)** I managed to eat it, and now I can go out to play!
   (B) Okay, I ate it, and now I am done; its time to go out and have some fun!
   (C) I finally ate it, and now I am free!

Unit 7
The Sound of Language

- Another type of rhyme is called **end rhyme.** With this type, the sounds at the ends of two lines rhyme.

  The branches tremble at the slightest **breeze**.

  It seems they're prepared for the first winter **freeze**.

Eyes to the Skies

Which sentence has end rhyme?

8. **(A)** Raindrops fall on the roof overhead. I hear them as I lie all snug in my bed.
   (B) Raindrops fall on the roof overhead. They keep me awake all night.
   (C) Raindrops fall on the roof overhead. Sometimes I think they will never stop.

9. **(A)** Lightning flashed, and then came the thunder. What else will happen, I wonder?
   (B) Lightning flashed, and then came the thunder. What a strange beginning to winter!
   (C) Lightning flashed, and then came the thunder. Will the next one be even stronger?

10. **(A)** Unlike me, flowers enjoy precipitation. They like to bloom in great amounts.
    (B) Unlike me, flowers enjoy precipitation. They even bloom in an explosion.
    (C) Unlike me, flowers enjoy precipitation. They even bloom in appreciation.

11. **(A)** The eye of a hurricane is quiet. The outer bands rage like a lion.
    (B) The eye of a hurricane is quiet. The outer bands rage like a riot.
    (C) The eye of a hurricane is quiet. The outer bands rage all night.

12. **(A)** What's going on with this typhoon? Is it supposed to calm down soon?
    (B) What's going on with this typhoon? I think this is the worst one.
    (C) What's going on with this typhoon? Isn't summer supposed to be more fun?

13. **(A)** The sun was concealed for days. It couldn't break through the trees.
    (B) The sun was concealed for days. It couldn't break through the haze.
    (C) The sun was concealed for days. It couldn't break through the rains.

Unit 7
The Sound of Language

Alliteration and assonance are other sound-of-language techniques you can use in sentences. You can use alliteration and assonance in poems and other kinds of writing, such as descriptive writing, to make it sound more interesting.

- **Alliteration** is the repetition of consonant sounds at the beginning of words.

  My **b**aby **b**rother was a **b**ouncing **b**undle of joy when he was **b**orn.

- **Assonance** is the repetition of the same vowel sound in different words in a sentence.

  The spect**a**cular c**a**stle st**a**nds on a cr**a**g.

African Wildlife

Which sentence uses alliteration?

14. **(A)** Hippos come out of the water at night.
    (B) A hippo's large jaws can smash through a boat.
    (C) The humongous hippo hides in the swamp.

15. **(A)** The crocodile has extremely strong jaws.
    (B) The creeping crocodile crawls through the cattails.
    (C) A crocodile and an alligator are not the same reptile.

16. **(A)** Leopards and lions lurk in the bushes.
    (B) A wide variety of mammals live in this part of the continent.
    (C) Despite what some may think, lions don't roam all throughout Africa.

17. **(A)** Gazelles dominate the Serengeti Plain.
    (B) Graceful gazelles graze in the grasslands.
    (C) Gazelles can jump straight up into the air.

18. **(A)** You may hear chummy chimpanzees make cheerful chatter.
    (B) Chimps live in groups that people call *troops*.
    (C) Chimps and monkeys are intelligent animals.

19. **(A)** Wildebeests migrate in a large circle each year.
    (B) They travel across the plains, savanna, and woodlands.
    (C) Wildebeests wander toward the woodlands.

Unit 7

The Sound of Language

Fantastic Castles

Which sentence uses assonance?

20. **(A)** A moat was known as a body of water that slowed approaching foes.
    (B) A drawbridge helped to protect the castle from invaders and let in those who were welcome.
    (C) Guards were stationed in towers to keep watch over the castle.

21. **(A)** With foresight, the queen said that every castle should supply defiant knights, and she was right.
    (B) A garrison was a group of soldiers that usually stayed in one place to defend the castle.
    (C) The knight's armor was very heavy and made of steel.

22. **(A)** The gatehouse defends the outer walls.
    (B) Concentric castles have rings of stone walls.
    (C) Proud guards stand in round towers that surround the castle.

23. **(A)** Archers shot their bows from behind stone walls called *parapets*.
    (B) Rocks were often dropped and hot tar was often slopped onto those who plot.
    (C) Hot sand burned intruders and stung their eyes.

24. **(A)** If a castle had a fish pond, it provided meals for many people.
    (B) A royal feast was a treat with courses of cheese, meat, and sweets.
    (C) They would have their food prepared with spices and garnished with eggs, fruits, and breads.

25. **(A)** Castles in those days were home to mostly noble folk.
    (B) Peasants worked on the castle grounds and in the fields.
    (C) Poets and musicians called *minstrels* played hornpipes and hurdy-gurdies.

26. **(A)** Including France, fancy castles still stand all over foreign lands.
    (B) How many rooms do you think there were in a typical castle?
    (C) Dunstanburgh Castle is one of northern England's most dramatic castles.

Unit 7
The Sound of Language

- **Onomatopoeia** is the use of a word whose sound refers to its meaning. Onomatopoeia imitates the sound of actions such as *crash, gurgle, zap, buzz, smack,* and *boom*. This sound-of-language technique is very useful in descriptive writing, narrative writing, and poetry because it can help readers to better understand how something sounds.

  The pancake batter **splattered** all over the stove top.

At the Amusement Park

Which sentence uses onomatopoeia?

27. **(A)** The balloon popped when it became overfilled with water.
    (B) The balloon broke when it became overfilled with water.

28. **(A)** The roar of the various roller coasters surrounded us on all sides.
    (B) We could hear the roller coasters everywhere we went.

29. **(A)** At the end of the ride, the cars came to a sudden stop.
    (B) When the ride was over, the cars screeched to a halt.

30. **(A)** We slurped ice-cold lemonade through curly straws.
    (B) We drank ice-cold lemonade through curly straws.

31. **(A)** Passengers ran to get in line when the trolley sounded its bell.
    (B) Passengers ran to get in line when the clanging of the trolley's bell was heard.

32. **(A)** Sausage sizzled on the vendor's grill.
    (B) The vendor cooked sausage on the grill.

33. **(A)** Riders gasped as they plunged down the slope.
    (B) Riders breathed deeply as they plunged down the slope.

34. **(A)** The ice cream slipped off my cone and landed on the ground.
    (B) The ice cream slipped off my cone and landed with a splat.

35. **(A)** The booming of the fireworks echoed throughout the park.
    (B) People could hear the fireworks everywhere in the park.

Unit 7
The Sound of Language

- **Repetition** can also add a special effect to your sentences. Repeated words and phrases can catch a reader's attention and add emphasis to the message you are trying to get across. This technique may be used in many kinds of writing, including speeches, narrative writing, and poetry.

  The ball is **going, going, going** . . . and it's gone!

  Yak, yak, yak—the reporter went **on and on**.

Which sentence has repetition?

36. **(A)** The band members stepped in unison.
    (B) Left, right, left, right, the marching band stepped together.

37. **(A)** Erica said to herself, "I really hope the car starts this time."
    (B) Erica said to herself, "Please, please, please let the car start."

38. **(A)** The airplane rose higher and higher until we could no longer see it.
    (B) The airplane rose so high that we could no longer see it.

39. **(A)** Breathe in to smell the cool, crisp air; breathe in to know that fall is finally here.
    (B) The smell of the leaves and the cool, crisp air lets me know that fall is finally here.

40. **(A)** You can call me any time, any place, for any reason.
    (B) You can call me whenever you want.

41. **(A)** Don't go anywhere else except the store.
    (B) Go straight to the store and come straight back.

42. **(A)** Recycle for your community, and recycle for your future; recycle today.
    (B) Recycling can benefit your community and help make for a brighter future.

43. **(A)** The coach joked and reminded us that the basketball is supposed to go through the basket.
    (B) "The basketball is supposed to go through, through, through the basket!" joked the coach.

44. **(A)** The leaky faucet would not stop dripping.
    (B) The leaky faucet went drip, drip, drip all night long.

Unit 8
Sentence Fluency

It is important to keep **sentence fluency** in mind as you are writing or revising your work. Too many short sentences or too many long sentences in a paragraph don't sound good together. Your sentences should also flow smoothly from one to the next.

- Write sentences that vary in length and type to make them sound much better when they are read aloud.
- Use **transition words** to move from one sentence to the next. Transition words show location *(at, below, near),* time *(after, today, when),* and order *(before, during, finally).*
- Remember that a comma and a conjunction *(and, but, or)* can also be used to combine short, related sentences and that other parts of sentences can be combined, such as participial and appositive phrases.

Pizza came to the United States in 1905. The first pizzeria opened in New York City. A *pizzeria* is a pizza shop. Hardly anyone knew about pizza. It became very popular.	→	Pizza came to the United States in 1905 **when** the first *pizzeria*, or pizza shop, opened in New York City. Hardly anyone knew about pizza**, but** it soon became very popular.

Which choice shows the best sentence fluency?

1. **(A)** Peregrine falcons once came extremely close to extinction. They ate other birds that were contaminated with a pesticide called DDT. About eighty percent of arctic peregrines died. Since DDT was banned in 1972, the falcons are making a comeback.

   (B) Peregrine falcons came close to extinction. They ate other birds. The birds were contaminated with a pesticide. The pesticide was called DDT. About eighty percent of arctic peregrines died. DDT was banned in 1972. The falcons are making a comeback.

   (C) Peregrine falcons once came extremely close to extinction because they ate other birds that were contaminated with a pesticide called DDT. About eighty percent of arctic peregrines died, but since DDT was banned in 1972, the falcons are making a comeback.

2. **(A)** Confucius was a philosopher in ancient China who studied Chinese religions and traditions, and then Confucius taught others what he had learned. He encouraged people to live together peacefully. He taught them to be honest and loyal. He also hoped people would respect their parents.

(B) Confucius was a philosopher in ancient China. He studied Chinese religions and traditions and then taught others what he had learned. He encouraged people to live together peacefully, be honest and loyal, and respect their parents.

(C) Confucius was a philosopher. He lived in ancient China and studied religions and traditions. He taught others what he learned. He thought people should live together in peace. He taught people to be honest, loyal, and respectful.

---

3. **(A)** It was the early 1900s. Millions of immigrants came to the United States. They arrived at Ellis Island in New York. They were given medical inspections. Those who passed could enter the country. They could go where they pleased. Those who had a serious illness were sent back home.

(B) In the early 1900s, millions of immigrants came to the United States, and when they got here, they arrived at Ellis Island in New York where they were given medical examinations. Those who passed could enter the country and go where they pleased, but those who had a serious illness were sent back home.

(C) In the early 1900s, millions of immigrants came to the United States. When they arrived at Ellis Island in New York, they were given medical inspections. Those who passed could enter the country and go where they pleased. Those who had a serious disease were sent back home.

---

4. **(A)** Male emperor penguins are good fathers. After the female lays an egg in the fall, she swims out to sea. The male stays behind to keep the egg warm by holding it on his feet all winter. He rarely takes time to eat!

(B) Male emperor penguins are good fathers. The female lays an egg. She lays it in the fall. Then she swims out to sea. The male stays behind. The male keeps the egg warm. He holds it on his feet all winter. He rarely eats!

(C) Male emperor penguins are good fathers. After the female lays an egg in the fall and swims out to sea, the male keeps the egg warm and does so by holding it on his feet all winter, and he rarely takes time to eat!

Unit 8

Sentence Fluency

Which choice shows the best sentence fluency?

5. **(A)** Jupiter is unique in several ways. Jupiter is the fifth planet from the sun. It is the largest planet and has the shortest day. Its day is only about ten hours long. Because Jupiter's days are so short, it means that Jupiter is spinning faster than any other planet. One of Jupiter's moons has more active volcanoes than any other known object in the solar system. This moon is called *Io*.

   (B) Jupiter, the fifth planet from the sun, is unique in several ways. First, Jupiter is the largest planet, and it also has the shortest day. A day on Jupiter is only about ten hours long; this means Jupiter is spinning faster than any other planet. Finally, one of Jupiter's moons, Io, has more active volcanoes than any other known object in the solar system.

   (C) Jupiter, the fifth planet from the sun, is unique in several ways. First, Jupiter is the largest planet. It also has the shortest day, which is only about ten hours long. This means Jupiter is spinning faster than any other planet. Finally, one of Jupiter's moons, Io, has more active volcanoes than any other known object in the solar system.

---

6. **(A)** The soundtrack adds a great deal to the overall effect of a movie by creating a particular feeling or atmosphere. The actors' dialogue usually takes up only one third of the soundtrack. The rest of the track is the score, or music, and sound effects.

   (B) The soundtrack adds a great deal to the overall effect of a movie. The soundtrack adds to the effect by creating a particular feeling or atmosphere. The actors' dialogue usually takes up only one third of the soundtrack, and the rest of the track is the score, or music, and sound effects.

   (C) The soundtrack adds to the overall effect of a movie. It adds to the overall effect by creating a particular feeling. Or it may create a particular atmosphere. The actors' dialogue takes up only one third of the soundtrack. The rest is the score and the sound effects.

---

7. **(A)** The first sharks may have existed millions of years ago. They existed before dinosaurs. Shark fossils were found on land. The land was under the sea in prehistoric times. Scientists can tell how old the fossils are. They know the age of the rocks in which they are found.

   (B) The first sharks may have existed millions of years before dinosaurs. Shark fossils have been found on land that was under the sea in prehistoric times, and scientists can tell how old the fossils are from the age of the rocks in which they are found.

   (C) The first sharks may have existed millions of years before dinosaurs. Shark fossils have been found on land under the sea in prehistoric times. Scientists can tell how old the fossils are from the age of the rocks in which they are found.

8. **(A)** In 1973 tennis player Billie Jean King won her most famous victory. The event was called "The Battle of the Sexes." In this match, Billie Jean faced off with male tennis player Bobby Riggs. Riggs had challenged King and taunted her with comments about men's athletic superiority over women. King easily won the match in straight sets!

(B) In 1973 a tennis player won her most famous victory in an event called "The Battle of the Sexes." The tennis player was Billie Jean King. In this match, Billie Jean faced off with male tennis player Bobby Riggs, who had challenged King and taunted her with comments about men's athletic superiority over women; King easily won the match in straight sets!

(C) In 1973 tennis player Billie Jean King won a famous victory. The event was called "The Battle of the Sexes." Billie Jean faced off with a male tennis player. His name was Bobby Riggs. Riggs had challenged King. He taunted her with comments about men's athletic superiority over women. King won the match in straight sets! She won easily.

---

9. **(A)** The hardest part of the human body is in your mouth. It's the enamel that covers your teeth. Enamel must be tough. It has to withstand many years of cutting and crushing. It also protects the inner parts of the tooth. It protects the softer parts of the tooth.

(B) The hardest part of the human body is in your mouth; it's the enamel that covers your teeth. Because it has to withstand many years of cutting and crushing, enamel must be tough. It also protects the inner, softer parts of the tooth.

(C) The hardest part of the human body is in your mouth; this hardest part is the enamel that covers your teeth. Enamel must be tough. Enamel has to withstand many years of cutting and crushing, and it also protects the inner parts of the tooth that are softer.

---

10. **(A)** The panpipe is a musical instrument. It is one of the most common instruments from the Andes region of South America. Panpipes are made of pieces of bamboo. The bamboo is cut to different lengths. The separate stalks of bamboo are bound together. They're bound with thin bamboo strips and string.

(B) The panpipe is one of the most common musical instruments, and they are from the Andes region of South America. Panpipes are made of pieces of bamboo cut to different lengths, and the separate stalks of bamboo are bound together with thin bamboo strips. The separate stalks are also bound together with string.

(C) The panpipe is one of the most common musical instruments from the Andes region of South America. Made of pieces of bamboo cut to different lengths, panpipes are bound together with thin bamboo strips and string.

Unit 9
Parallelism

Parallelism refers to making parts of a sentence parallel, or making them match in form. Two or more words, phrases, or clauses should be parallel when they have the same function in a sentence, relate to the same thing, and express ideas that are equal in purpose.

- To be parallel, adjectives and adverbs that modify the same word must have the same degree of comparison.

  Not Parallel: Julio was the strongest, more gifted athlete on the field.

  Parallel: Julio was the **strongest**, **most gifted** athlete on the field.

  Not Parallel: Our team played fiercely but fair.

  Parallel: Our team played **fiercely** but **fairly**.

- Verbs that have the same subject must be the same tense and form.

  Not Parallel: Marisa is running and kicked the ball toward the goal.

  Parallel: Marisa **ran** and **kicked** the ball toward the goal.

All-American Athlete

Decide whether the underlined words should be changed.

Jim Thorpe was one of the (1) talented, most well-rounded athletes to ever live. Thorpe, a Native American, first displayed his exceptional and (2) diverse athletic skill as a student at the Carlisle Indian School. Later, at the 1912 Olympic Games, Thorpe won gold medals in the pentathlon and decathlon events. As a result of these victories, many people respected and commonly (3) recognize Thorpe as the greatest all-around athlete of the twentieth century. Thorpe played professional baseball and football and even (4) had won three unofficial world championships with the Canton Bulldogs in 1916, 1917, and 1919. His honors are numerous and (5) deserved. As a special tribute, the town where he is buried was renamed Jim Thorpe, Pennsylvania.

1. **(A)** No change
   (B) Change to *most talented*

2. **(A)** No change
   (B) Change to *more diverse*

3. **(A)** No change
   (B) Change to *recognized*

4. **(A)** No change
   (B) Change to *won*

5. **(A)** No change
   (B) Change to *most deserved*

Unit 9

Parallelism

Dominant Traits

Traits are physical characteristics determined by genes. Certain traits are dominant, which means they are stronger and **(6)** more likely to appear. For example, dark, **(7)** curlier hair is dominant over light, straight hair. Also, if you can roll your tongue easily and **(8)** more quickly, you have inherited a dominant trait. The genes for dimples, whether they're shallow or **(9)** deep, are also dominant. If you touch or **(10)** are looking at your earlobes and **(11)** noticed they hang freely, you have the dominant gene for earlobes. Did you ever notice whether your hairline is **(12)** straightest or pointed? Your hairline is most likely to be pointed, even if it is a **(13)** smaller or subtle peak, because the genes for this trait are dominant. **(14)** Stretch out your hand, and look at your pinky. Does it bend slightly inward toward your ring finger? If so, you have the dominant gene.

6. **(A)** No change
   (B) Change to *most likely*

7. **(A)** No change
   (B) Change to *curly*

8. **(A)** No change
   (B) Change to *quickly*

9. **(A)** No change
   (B) Change to *deeper*

10. **(A)** No change
    (B) Change to *look*

11. **(A)** No change
    (B) Change to *notice*

12. **(A)** No change
    (B) Change to *straight*

13. **(A)** No change
    (B) Change to *small*

14. **(A)** No change
    (B) Change to *Stretching*

Unit 9
Parallelism

- In a series of three or more items, the words or phrases should be parallel in form. For example, if the first two items are adjectives, the other items must also be adjectives. Be careful not to place two adjectives and a verb or verb phrase in a series as if they were parallel ideas.

  Not Parallel: My computer is old, slow, and makes a lot of noise.

  Parallel: My computer is **old**, **slow**, and **noisy**.

An Apple a Day

Decide whether the underlined words should be changed.

Apples are popular, widely grown, and (15) have a lot of nutrition. They (16) contain neither fat nor sodium and are a great alternative to cookies or potato chips. They also contain fiber, which helps to reduce cholesterol and (17) is preventing heart disease. Recent studies show that apples also strengthen the lungs. Apples come in many varieties, so a person who is in the mood for a snack (18) has many options. Granny Smith apples are bright green, tart, and (19) crisp. Red Delicious apples are mildly sweet, crunchy, and (20) have a bright red color. Apples can be used in salads, pies, and (21) to make sauces. The average person in the United States eats about one apple per week, but experts recommend eating one apple every day to reap all of the nutritional benefits.

15. **(A)** No change
    (B) Change to *nutritious*

16. **(A)** No change
    (B) Change to *have contained*

17. **(A)** No change
    (B) Change to *prevent*

18. **(A)** No change
    (B) Change to *have*

19. **(A)** No change
    (B) Change to *have crispness*

20. **(A)** No change
    (B) Change to *bright red*

21. **(A)** No change
    (B) Change to *sauces*

Unit 9
Parallelism

A Man Ahead of His Time

Leonardo da Vinci may be best known as the person who painted *Mona Lisa* in the 1500s, but he was much more than a painter. He was an artist, a scientist, and (22) liked to invent things. He not only created classic and (23) most beautiful works of art but also (24) did invent complex, (25) practical devices. For example, da Vinci (26) had imagined and designed a flying machine and an armored tank hundreds of years before they became a reality. The fact that these inventions were neither built nor used until several centuries later shows that he was insightful, ingenious, and (27) had creativity. His achievements also led to the popular expression "renaissance man," which refers to a person who is successful, studious, and (28) multitalented.

22. **(A)** No change
(B) Change to *an inventor*

23. **(A)** No change
(B) Change to *beautiful*

24. **(A)** No change
(B) Change to *invented*

25. **(A)** No change
(B) Change to *more practical*

26. **(A)** No change
(B) Change to *imagined*

27. **(A)** No change
(B) Change to *creative*

28. **(A)** No change
(B) Change to *has many talents*

Unit 9
Parallelism

- Use the same preposition to introduce words or phrases in a series. The words following each preposition should also be in the same form.

  Not Parallel: I use the Internet to locate information and for playing games.

  Parallel: I use the Internet **to locate information** and **to play games**.

It is only necessary to repeat the preposition if the meaning is unclear without it or if the first two items in a series of three or more already include a preposition.

  Not Parallel: He asked us to read, to write, and listen carefully.

  Parallel: He asked us **to read**, **to write**, and **to listen** carefully.

Gabriela Mistral

Decide whether the underlined words should be changed.

Gabriela Mistral loved to read, to write, and (29) to sing when she was a child. As a young schoolteacher, she worked on improving her teaching and (30) on finding ways to make learning fun for her students. She often took the children outside to enjoy and (31) for studying nature. Her goals were to improve schools and (32) to make books more available to children in Chile and Mexico. She also wrote poems that were sad and (33) emotional. In 1945 she became the first Latin American to be awarded the Nobel Prize for Literature. Gabriela Mistral will be remembered as a gifted poet, an accomplished teacher, and (34) for her success as a diplomat.

29. **(A)** No change
    (B) Change to *singing*

30. **(A)** No change
    (B) Change to *to find*

31. **(A)** No change
    (B) Change to *to study*

32. **(A)** No change
    (B) Change to *making*

33. **(A)** No change
    (B) Change to *had a lot of emotion*

34. **(A)** No change
    (B) Change to *a successful diplomat*

Unit 9
Parallelism

Indian Leader Mahatma Gandhi

Mahatma Gandhi is known throughout the world for his quest to do away with oppressive laws and customs and (35) as a person who worked to gain India's independence from Great Britain. Born in 1869, Gandhi became dedicated to nonviolence, to tolerance, and (36) justice at an early age. He went to law school in London, eventually using his education to protest anti-Indian laws in South Africa and (37) for fighting discrimination. In India, Gandhi turned his attention to helping the "Untouchables," a group of people who were poor, uneducated, and (38) suffered terrible treatment. His goal was to help boost their self-esteem and (39) to get other social classes to accept them. As a leader, he was powerful, assertive, and (40) had heroic qualities. These qualities became more and more evident as he worked to liberate India and (41) to urge nonviolent campaigns. Although he was tragically assassinated in 1948, Gandhi will always be a symbol of peace, justice, and (42) for sacrificing.

35. **(A)** No change
(B) Change to *for his work*

36. **(A)** No change
(B) Change to *to justice*

37. **(A)** No change
(B) Change to *to fight discrimination*

38. **(A)** No change
(B) Change to *miserable*

39. **(A)** No change
(B) Change to *getting other social classes*

40. **(A)** No change
(B) Change to *heroic*

41. **(A)** No change
(B) Change to *urging*

42. **(A)** No change
(B) Change to *sacrifice*

The Third LAP

Language Activity Pages

A. Exercising Your Skill

You have been learning about the sound of language, sentence fluency, and parallelism. Number your paper from 1 to 4. Then answer the following questions about what you have learned.

1. Which sound of language is characterized by the repetition of consonant sounds at the beginning of words?
   (A) alliteration **(B)** assonance **(C)** onomatopoeia
2. If a line of text has words that rhyme within the line and not just at the end, what is that called?
   (A) repetition **(B)** end rhyme **(C)** internal rhyme
3. What is the best way to achieve sentence fluency in your writing?
   (A) Make all the sentences the same type and length.
   (B) Use a variety of sentence types and lengths.
   (C) Try to use either all long or all short sentences.
4. In order for two verbs in a sentence to be parallel, what must happen?
   (A) Both verbs have to be in the active voice.
   (B) Both verbs must be next to one another.
   (C) Both verbs have to be the same tense and form.

B. Expanding Your Skill

Read each sentence. Number your paper from 1 to 4. Then choose the item that does *not* have errors in parallelism.

1. **(A)** Two things I like to do are eating out and to go to the movies.
   (B) Two things I like to do are eating out and going to the movies.
2. **(A)** Little red lights run to the end of the long, narrow aisle in the movie theater.
   (B) Little red lights run to the end of the longer, narrow aisle in the movie theater.
3. **(A)** Just before the movie starts, people quickly and most quietly take their seats.
   (B) Just before the movie starts, people quickly and quietly take their seats.
4. **(A)** The popcorn is hot, fresh, and has a lot of butter.
   (B) The popcorn is hot, fresh, and buttery.

C. Exploring Language

Poetry Read the following poem. Number your paper from 1 to 12. Choose a word from the box to fill in each blank and create the sound of language that will make the poem more interesting to read.

slowly	instead	do	grow	chews	matter
clatter	shoes	see	head	moos	way

There's a dinosaur in my basement; I tell you it's true.
If you happened to be me, what would you _____?
When the time is right and the light's not too dim,
Step _____ down the stairs and you'll certainly see him
For it's usually around this exact time of day,
He eats just about anything that gets in his _____.
This silly creature must think everything's yummy
For there's never enough to fill his ol' tummy
As sure as the dairy cow _____ and moos,
The dinosaur chews and _____ but can't stomach old _____.
What if we give him some steak _____ ?
My parents disbelieve me, saying it's all in my _____.
But this I know: one day he'll _____ too big to hide
Then no longer will he be able to stay inside.
With a bang and a _____ something will shatter.
My parents would go down to see what's the _____.
Ponder a moment with me, and I'm sure you'll agree
Oh, what a shock it would be, definitely a sight to _____—
The looks on their faces upon hearing its roar
And coming face to face with a true dinosaur!

D. Expressing Yourself

Choose one of these activities. When you are finished, give your paper to your teacher.

1. Read the sentences below. Rewrite and combine the sentences to make one complete paragraph using transition words where needed to improve fluency.
   Get out some bread. Make a few sandwiches.
   Choose several pieces of fresh fruit. Pack your picnic in a cooler or a basket.
   Grab a big soft blanket to rest on. Don't forget to take a kite.
   Enjoy your afternoon at the park!

2. WORK with a PARTNER Look through some of your favorite books for passages that contain good examples of sentence fluency. Read a passage aloud with your partner, and then discuss the effectiveness of the passage. Write a paragraph explaining what characteristics of the sentences made the passage fluent.

Unit 10

Sentence Problems

A **fragment** is a group of words that is written as a sentence but is missing a subject, a predicate, or both. A fragment is incorrect because it does *not* express a complete thought. Don't be fooled by subordinate clauses. Although they may have a subject and a verb, they are not complete thoughts.

Do not resemble their parents after they hatch. (missing a subject)

The frog sitting on top of the lily pad. (missing a predicate)

From one to the other in search of food. (missing both)

The Underground Railroad

Decide whether each sentence is missing a subject, a predicate, or both.

1. The railroad, even though it was not an actual railroad with cars and tracks.
   (A) subject **(B)** predicate **(C)** both

2. A network of secret routes and safe houses to help slaves escape to freedom.
   (A) subject **(B)** predicate **(C)** both

3. Were owned by whites and free blacks who opposed slavery.
   (A) subject **(B)** predicate **(C)** both

4. Often traveling under the cloak of darkness at night.
   (A) subject **(B)** predicate **(C)** both

5. Followed rivers and the North Star, part of the Big Dipper constellation.
   (A) subject **(B)** predicate **(C)** both

6. Ate and rested to prepare for the night's journey.
   (A) subject **(B)** predicate **(C)** both

7. A lantern on a pitching post outside of a house.
   (A) subject **(B)** predicate **(C)** both

8. Usually meant that a warm welcome and a hot meal were waiting.
   (A) subject **(B)** predicate **(C)** both

9. Traveling on foot and later in wagons.
   (A) subject **(B)** predicate **(C)** both

10. Settled in a free state in the North or went on to Canada.
   (A) subject **(B)** predicate **(C)** both

Unit 10

Sentence Problems

A **run-on sentence** is two or more sentences that are incorrectly written as one complete sentence. To correct this problem, write the sentences separately, or combine them by using a comma and a conjunction *(and, but, or)*, a semicolon, or a subordinating conjunction *(because, that, when)*.

Run-on: Hair color is a trait that has many variations it is controlled by several gene pairs.

Correct: Hair color is a trait that has many variations **because** it is controlled by several gene pairs.

Correct: Hair color is a trait that has many variations**. It** is controlled by several gene pairs.

Mayan Calendar

Which is the correct way to fix each run-on sentence?

11. The Mayan people invented a calendar system it was based on cycles of the sun and moon.
    (A) The Mayan people invented a calendar system; it was based on cycles of the sun and moon.
    (B) The Mayan people invented a calendar system but it was based on cycles of the sun and moon.
    (C) Neither of these

12. Their system included several calendars they used them for different purposes.
    (A) Their system included several calendars so they used them for different purposes.
    (B) Their system included several calendars. They used them for different purposes.
    (C) Neither of these

13. One calendar was based on 260 days another was based on 365 days.
    (A) One calendar was based on 260 days, another was based on 365 days.
    (B) One calendar was based on 260 days, and another was based on 365 days.
    (C) Neither of these

14. The 260-day calendar was used for planting and harvesting corn the 365-day calendar, called the *Haab*, was based on Earth's orbit around the sun.
    (A) The 260-day calendar was used for planting and harvesting corn, the 365-day calendar, called the *Haab*, was based on Earth's orbit around the sun.
    (B) The 260-day calendar was used for planting and harvesting corn. The 365-day calendar, called the *Haab*, was based on Earth's orbit around the sun.
    (C) Neither of these

Unit 10
Sentence Problems

A **modifier** is a word or a phrase that describes another word or phrase. When a modifier is used or placed incorrectly, it may appear that the modifier is not describing anything, or it can be hard to tell which word the modifier is supposed to be describing.

- A **dangling modifier** is a group of words that does not seem to sensibly modify anything in a sentence.

  Dangling: Working late into the night, the project was finally finished.

  Correct: Working late into the night, Yu-Ling finally finished the project.
  (Working late into the night now modifies the subject *Yu-Ling.)*

- A **misplaced modifier** is a group of words that modifies the wrong word or appears to modify more than one word in a sentence.

  Misplaced: These are some tips for staying safe from our doctor.

  Correct: These are some tips **from our doctor** for staying safe.
  (from our doctor now correctly modifies the subject *tips)*

Which sentence does not have an error in the use of modifiers?

15. **(A)** After reading the library books, we put them away.
    (B) After reading the library books, they were put away.

16. **(A)** The tourists took a picture of the statue walking down the street.
    (B) The tourists walking down the street took a picture of the statue.

17. **(A)** Toyah could see a deer grazing in the distance with her binoculars.
    (B) With her binoculars, Toyah could see a deer grazing in the distance.

18. **(A)** Passing through the city, we saw a parade in procession.
    (B) Passing through the city, a long parade could be seen in procession.

19. **(A)** I noticed Canada geese flying north while delivering newspapers.
    (B) While delivering newspapers, I noticed Canada geese flying north.

20. **(A)** On his first visit to the zoo, a gorilla almost got loose.
    (B) On his first visit to the zoo, Seth said a gorilla almost got loose.

21. **(A)** Dad saw the raccoon digging through the trash.
    (B) Digging through the trash, Dad saw the raccoon.

22. **(A)** Pulling into the driveway, the light shined into our bedroom.
(B) Pulling into the driveway, the car's lights shined into our bedroom.

23. **(A)** Flying too close to a tree, we saw the kite had gotten stuck.
(B) We saw that the kite flying too close to a tree had gotten stuck.

24. **(A)** Reaching into the bushes, a rabbit darted out from behind them.
(B) Reaching into the bushes, I noticed a rabbit dart out from behind them.

25. **(A)** I must have left the umbrella that I was carrying inside the restaurant.
(B) I must have left the umbrella inside the restaurant that I was carrying.

26. **(A)** Stepping up to the plate, the softball came quickly toward Letitia.
(B) The softball came quickly toward Letitia as she stepped up to the plate.

27. **(A)** Huffing and puffing, we pushed the stalled car all the way up the street.
(B) Huffing and puffing, the stalled car was pushed all the way up the street.

28. **(A)** Running to catch the bus, Enrique accidentally dropped his books.
(B) Running to catch the bus, the books were accidentally dropped.

29. **(A)** In reviewing the videotape, several errors were made.
(B) In reviewing the videotape, the team found they had made several errors.

30. **(A)** I served sandwiches to the hungry guests on paper plates.
(B) I served sandwiches on paper plates to the hungry guests.

31. **(A)** Driving south, Mr. Hayashi noted that the land was not as flat.
(B) Driving south, the land was not as flat.

32. **(A)** Turning off the lights, the room looked totally different.
(B) Turning off the lights, Janice thought the room looked totally different.

33. **(A)** I found a five-dollar bill in the ditch walking home.
(B) Walking home, I found a five-dollar bill in the ditch.

Unit 10

Sentence Problems

The word a pronoun refers to is called its **antecedent.** When you use a pronoun, be sure it clearly refers to its antecedent.

- A sentence is unclear if a pronoun could refer to more than one antecedent. Sometimes you must repeat a noun or rewrite a sentence to avoid confusion.

  Charlotte Bronte wrote a novel about a young woman. She was a governess. (It is not clear if *She* refers to *Charlotte Bronte* or to *a young woman*.)

  Charlotte Bronte wrote a novel about a young woman. **The young woman** was a governess.

- Be especially careful when you use the pronoun *they* because it may not be clear to whom *they* refers. In that case, it is best to rewrite the sentence without *they*.

  Unclear: They have five books by Bronte at the school library.

  Clear: **The school library** has five books by Bronte.

Does the underlined pronoun in each sentence clearly refer to its antecedent?

34. Mr. Ortega spoke to Neil about the class project. He was enthusiastic.
(A) Yes, the antecedent is clear.
(B) No, the antecedent is unclear.

35. Neil had an idea. He wanted to explain how plants make food.
(A) Yes, the antecedent is clear.
(B) No, the antecedent is unclear.

36. Mr. Ortega said that they have a special exhibit about plant life at the Natural History Museum.
(A) Yes, the antecedent is clear.
(B) No, the antecedent is unclear.

37. The students in Mr. Ortega's class drew diagrams of plant leaves. Mr. Ortega thought they were good.
(A) Yes, the antecedent is clear.
(B) No, the antecedent is unclear.

38. Plants produce sugar. They use it as food.
(A) Yes, the antecedent is clear.
(B) No, the antecedent is unclear.

39. A plant also produces oxygen. It is important to humans.
(A) Yes, the antecedent is clear.
(B) No, the antecedent is unclear.

Unit 10

Sentence Problems

40. Malcolm went to the museum with Neil. He needed some more information.
(A) Yes, the antecedent is clear.
(B) No, the antecedent is unclear.

41. They had microscopes set up for visitors to use.
(A) Yes, the antecedent is clear.
(B) No, the antecedent is unclear.

42. The museum volunteers showed Malcolm and Neil how to use the microscopes. They were powerful.
(A) Yes, the antecedent is clear.
(B) No, the antecedent is unclear.

43. Neil looked into the microscope. After adjusting it carefully, he could see guard cells.
(A) Yes, the antecedent is clear.
(B) No, the antecedent is unclear.

44. The guard cells control the opening and closing of the leaves' "mouths," or stomata. They shrink and swell to allow the stomata to either take in carbon dioxide and water or to let out oxygen.
(A) Yes, the antecedent is clear.
(B) No, the antecedent is unclear.

45. In Mr. Ortega's class, they learned that plants can only make food if water enters cells that contain chlorophyll.
(A) Yes, the antecedent is clear.
(B) No, the antecedent is unclear.

46. Mr. Ortega asked Neil to report his findings to the class. He walked to the front of the room.
(A) Yes, the antecedent is clear.
(B) No, the antecedent is unclear.

47. Malcolm presented the findings with Neil. He talked about photosynthesis.
(A) Yes, the antecedent is clear.
(B) No, the antecedent is unclear.

48. Malcolm and Neil gave the students tiny plants to take home. They were happy.
(A) Yes, the antecedent is clear.
(B) No, the antecedent is unclear.

Unit 11
Expanding Sentences

Adding details to sentences can help to make your writing less choppy and more interesting. Don't overload your sentences with details, though. Add details only when they give the reader a clearer picture of what's happening.

- One way to expand sentences is by adding participial phrases. Remember that a participle is a verb form that ends with *-ed* or *-ing*.

  The player is our catcher.

  The player **rounding the bases** is our catcher.

- A second way to expand sentences is to add an appositive phrase.

  The Vikings thrived for centuries.

  The Vikings**, brave warriors and explorers,** thrived for centuries.

Play Ball!

Which expanded sentence includes a participial or an appositive phrase?

1. The pitcher looks for signals from the catcher.
   (A) The pitcher stares intently and looks for signals from the catcher.
   (B) The pitcher, staring intently, looks for signals from the catcher.
   (C) The pitcher looks intently for signals from the catcher.

---

2. The batter swung awkwardly.
   (A) The batter swung awkwardly at the fastball.
   (B) Awkwardly but swiftly, the batter swung at the fastball.
   (C) The batter, our last hope for victory, swung awkwardly.

---

3. The outfielder missed the fly ball.
   (A) The outfielder missed the fly ball when he lost it in the sun.
   (B) Blinded by the sun, the outfielder missed the fly ball.
   (C) The bright sun caused the outfielder to miss the fly ball.

---

4. The manager watched another runner score.
   (A) The manager, holding his head in his hands, watched another runner score.
   (B) The manager watched another runner round the bases and score.
   (C) The manager watched in amazement as another runner scored.

---

5. Everyone enjoyed the seventh-inning stretch.
   (A) Singing enthusiastically, everyone enjoyed the seventh-inning stretch.
   (B) Everyone except for the losing team enjoyed the seventh-inning stretch.
   (C) Everyone enjoyed the seventh-inning stretch because they were tired of sitting.

Unit 11

Expanding Sentences

- You can also expand sentences by adding a dependent clause.

  Rachel Carson sold her first story.

  Rachel Carson sold her first story **when she was only ten years old**.
- Another way to expand sentences is to add an adjective clause, a type of dependent clause. Do *not* use commas around an adjective clause that is necessary to the meaning of the sentence.

  Sequoya was a Native American **who developed the Cherokee alphabet**.
- Use commas around an adjective clause only when it is *not* essential to the sentence's meaning.

  The first Native American newspaper, **which was written in Cherokee and English,** was published in 1828.

Which expanded sentence includes a dependent clause?

6. Sequoya was born in Tennessee.
   (A) Sequoya was born in Tennessee, and that is where he spent most of his life.
   (B) Sequoya was born in Tennessee, a southeastern state, and he died in Mexico.
   (C) Sequoya was born in Tennessee, where his ancestors had lived for thousands of years.

7. Sequoya had a hunting accident.
   (A) Sequoya's hunting accident, a terrible tragedy, left him lame.
   (B) Sequoya was lame after his hunting accident.
   (C) Sequoya knew that his hunting accident would leave him lame.

8. Sequoya couldn't read or write.
   (A) Sequoya, who spoke several languages, couldn't read or write.
   (B) Sequoya couldn't read or write, so he invented an alphabet.
   (C) Sequoya, amazed by the white man's written language, couldn't read or write.

9. Thousands of Cherokees died in the 1830s.
   (A) Thousands of Cherokees died in the 1830s and were forced off of their land.
   (B) Walking 800 miles to Oklahoma, thousands of Cherokees died in the 1830s.
   (C) Thousands of Cherokees died in the 1830s when they walked the "Trail of Tears."

10. The Cherokee people were grateful to Sequoya.
    (A) The Cherokee people were grateful to Sequoya for preserving their culture.
    (B) The Cherokee people, and other Native Americans, were grateful to Sequoya.
    (C) The Cherokee people, whose culture was preserved, were grateful to Sequoya.

The Last LAP
Language Activity Pages

A. Exercising Your Skill

You have been learning about different kinds of sentence problems and how to expand sentences. Answer these questions about what you have learned.

1. What is a group of words that is written as a sentence but is missing a subject, a predicate, or both called?
   (A) run-on sentence **(B)** fragment **(C)** misplaced modifier
2. If a modifier does not sensibly describe another word in a sentence, what kind of problem does this sentence have?
   (A) misplaced modifier **(B)** unclear antecedent **(C)** dangling modifier
3. Which of the following is *not* a way to expand a sentence?
   (A) add a participial phrase **(B)** add an appositive **(C)** add a comma
4. To what kind of noun should the pronoun *they* always refer?
   (A) singular **(B)** plural **(C)** it doesn't matter

B. Expanding Your Skill

Read each sentence. Identify the problem that each one has.

1. The runners warming up for the track meet.
   (A) run-on **(B)** fragment **(C)** misplaced modifier
2. Singing at the top of her voice, the volume was much too loud.
   (A) unclear antecedent **(B)** dangling modifier **(C)** fragment
3. We rode our bikes to the top of the hill the view was incredible.
   (A) misplaced modifier **(B)** dangling modifier **(C)** run-on
4. Yolanda gave Martha her apple. She didn't want it.
   (A) unclear antecedent **(B)** run-on **(C)** misplaced modifier
5. I could clearly see a bear with my own two eyes in the distance.
   (A) misplaced modifier **(B)** fragment **(C)** dangling modifier
6. Went running as fast as I could back to the cabin to tell everyone what I saw.
   (A) run-on **(B)** unclear antecedent **(C)** fragment

C. Exploring Language

Narrative Writing Read the paragraph below from a narrative story. Then number your paper from 1 to 6. Use the phrases and clauses in the box to expand the sentences in the paragraph when possible.

(A) , the twins,
(B) after they got home from school
(C) Hoping to win concert tickets,
(D) the Mississippi and Missouri Rivers
(E) When their favorite group performs,
(F) excited about the contest,

Janelle and Trey **(1)**_____ turned on the radio **(2)**_____. **(3)**_____ they listened and waited for the next trivia question. Finally, the disc jockey, **(4)**_____ read the next question: What are America's two longest rivers? Janelle knew the answer! She got through to the station and gave them her answer, **(5)**_____. **(6)**_____ Janelle and Trey will be sitting in the front row!

D. Expressing Yourself

Choose one of these activities. When you are finished, give your paper to your teacher.

1. WORK with a PARTNER Play a sentence-building game with a partner. Take turns writing one word at a time to create a sentence. Use clues, such as including a comma after your word, when you want to add an appositive or other special element to the sentence. Make sure you include participial phrases, dependent clauses, and appositives in your sentences. Avoid run-ons, fragments, dangling or misplaced modifiers, and unclear antecedents.

2. Pick an object in the room, and think of different ways you can describe it using the sentence-expanding techniques you have practiced. Start with a simple sentence, and then build on it. See how many variations you can come up with. For example:

    The jeans lay on the floor.

    The ripped jeans lay on the floor.

    The ripped jeans lay on the floor until Janelle cleaned her room.

    The ripped jeans lay on the floor until Janelle, Trey's sister, cleaned her room.

SENTENCES Scope and Sequence • *Specific Skill Series for Language Arts*

Unit/Level	Level A	Level B	Level C	Level D	Level E	Level F	Level G	Level H
Unit 1	Building Sentences	Building Sentences	Building Sentences	Building Sentences	Building Sentences	Building Sentences	Building Sentences	Building Sentences
Unit 2	Building Sentences	Building Sentences	Building Sentences	Building Sentences	Building Sentences	Building Sentences	Combining Sentences	Combining Sentences
Unit 3	Building Sentences	Building Sentences	Building Sentences	Building Sentences	Building Sentences	Building Sentences	Combining Sentences	Combining Sentences
Unit 4	Building Sentences	Building Sentences	Building Sentences	Building Sentences	Building Sentences	Building Sentences	The Sound of Language	The Sound of Language
Unit 5	Building Sentences	Combining Sentences	Building Sentences	Building Sentences	Combining Sentences	Combining Sentences	Sentence Fluency	Sentence Fluency
Unit 6	Combining Sentences	Combining Sentences	Building Sentences	Building Sentences	Combining Sentences	Combining Sentences	Parallelism	Parallelism
Unit 7	Combining Sentences	Correct Word Order in a Sentence	Combining Sentences	Combining Sentences	Combining Sentences	The Sound of Language	Parallelism	Parallelism
Unit 8	Putting Words in the Correct Order	Parallelism	Combining Sentences	Combining Sentences	The Sound of Language	Sentence Fluency	Sentence Problems	Sentence Problems
Unit 9	Agreement with Verbs and Adjectives	Sentence Problems	Combining Sentences	Combining Sentences	Sentence Fluency	Parallelism	Sentence Problems	Sentence Problems
Unit 10	Sentence Problems	Sentence Problems	Combining Sentences	Correct Word Order	Parallelism	Sentence Problems	Expanding Sentences	Expanding Sentences
Unit 11	Adding Prepositional Phrases	Adding Prepositional Phrases	Combining Sentences	The Sound of Language	Sentence Problems	Expanding Sentences	Diagramming Sentences	Diagramming Sentences
Unit 12			Correct Word Order	Sentence Fluency	Expanding Sentences			
Unit 13			Parallelism	Parallelism				
Unit 14			Sentence Fluency	Sentence Problems				
Unit 15			Sentence Problems	Sentence Problems				
Unit 16			Sentence Problems	Sentence Problems				